WELCOME TO MY COUNTRY

Welcome to
ALGERIA

Gareth Stevens Publishing
A WORLD ALMANAC EDUCATION GROUP COMPANY

Written by
CHIN OI LING

Edited by
KATHARINE BROWN-CARPENTER

Edited in USA by
JENETTE DONOVAN GUNTLY

Designed by
BENSON TAN

Picture research by
THOMAS KHOO
JOSHUA ANG

First published in North America in 2006 by
Gareth Stevens Publishing
A WRC Media Company
330 West Olive Street, Suite 100
Milwaukee, Wisconsin 53212 USA

Please visit our web site at
www.garethstevens.com
For a free color catalog describing
Gareth Stevens Publishing's list of high-quality
books and multimedia programs,
call 1-800-542-2595 (USA) or
1-800-387-3178 (Canada).
Gareth Stevens Publishing's fax: (414) 332-3567.

© **MARSHALL CAVENDISH INTERNATIONAL (ASIA)**
PRIVATE LIMITED 2005
Originated and designed by
Times Editions—Marshall Cavendish
An imprint of Marshall Cavendish International (Asia) Pte Ltd
A member of Times Publishing Limited
Times Centre, 1 New Industrial Road
Singapore 536196
http://www.marshallcavendish.com/genref

Library of Congress Cataloging-in-Publication Data
Chin, Oi Ling.
Welcome to Algeria / Chin Oi Ling.
p. cm. — (Welcome to my country)
Includes bibliographical references and index.
ISBN 0-8368-3132-2 (lib. bdg.)
1. Algeria—Juvenile literature. I. Title. II. Series.
DT275.C67   2005
965—dc22   2005042622

Printed in Singapore

1 2 3 4 5 6 7 8 9 09 08 07 06 05

PICTURE CREDITS
Agence France Presse: 15 (top), 29
Art Directors & TRIP Photo Library: 34
Corbis: 3 (bottom), 9, 14, 15 (bottom),
    21, 22, 30, 31, 38, 39
Focus Team—Italy: 1, 4, 10, 41, 43
HBL Network: cover, 2, 3 (top & center),
    5, 7, 8 (both), 11, 15 (center),16, 17,
    18 (bottom), 19, 20, 23 (both), 24, 25,
    26, 27, 28, 32, 33, 35, 36, 37, 40, 45
The Hutchison Library: 18 (top)
North Wind Picture Archives: 12
Still Pictures: 6
Audrius Tomonis – www.banknotes.com:
    44 (both)
Topham Picturepoint: 13

Digital Scanning by Superskill Graphics Pte Ltd

Contents

Words that appear in the glossary are printed in **boldface** type the first time they occur in the text.

Welcome to Algeria!

Algeria, the tenth-largest country in the world, is located in northwest Africa. The Sahara Desert covers much of the country. Algeria's past rulers, such as the Arabs and French, have influenced many parts of Algerian life, including its architecture and music. Let's explore Algeria and learn about its people!

Opposite: A **nomad** stands in the Sahara Desert in Algeria. The man has wrapped his face in cloth to keep sand from entering his nose and mouth.

Below: Algiers is the capital city of Algeria. It is also the nation's largest city.

The Flag of Algeria

Algeria's flag has a green and a white rectangle. The color green stands for the religion of Islam. White stands for **purity**. Since the 1100s, the moon and star have been symbols of the Islamic religion. The color red stands for freedom.

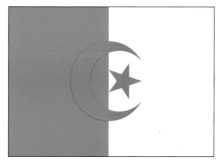

The Land

Algeria is the second-largest country in Africa. It has an area of 919,595 square miles (2,381,740 square kilometers). Algeria is surrounded by the nations of Morocco, Western Sahara, Mauritania, Mali, Niger, Libya, and Tunisia. The Mediterranean Sea is to the north. Most people live in northern Algeria in the Tell region, which includes hills, plains, valleys, and the Tell Atlas Mountains.

Below: The Aurès Mountains form part of the Saharan Atlas Mountains in northern Algeria.

The Chelif River, Algeria's longest and most important river, starts in the Saharan Atlas Mountains, which are south of the High **Plateau**. The river is about 450 miles (725 kilometers) long.

Most of southern Algeria is covered by the Sahara Desert, which is divided into two regions. The Great Western **Erg** consists mostly of sand dunes. The Great Eastern Erg is made up of sand dunes and the Ahaggar Mountains. The highest peak in Algeria is Mount Tahat. It is located in the Ahaggar Mountains and is 9,852 feet (3,003 meters) high.

Climate

The climate in Algeria varies from region to region. In the northern part of the country, summer temperatures average 70° to 75° Fahrenheit (21° to 24° Celsius). In the High Plateau, temperatures can reach 100° F (38° C). A hot, sandy wind called a sirocco also blows through this region during the summer. In the Sahara Desert, the climate is very hot in the summer. Winter temperatures in Algeria are mild and rarely fall below freezing.

Above:
The Tuaregs are nomads who are **descendants** of the Berbers. They live mainly in the Sahara Desert.

Left: The climate on the Algerian coast is good for growing crops. The country's coastal areas also receive the most rain.

Left: The scimitar oryx (*left*) and the dama gazelle were **native** to Algeria. Today, both kinds of animals are **extinct** in Algeria.

Plants and Animals

The few remaining forests in Algeria can be found in the mountain regions. Shrubs such as rosemary grow in the northern part of the country, while brushwood and esparto grass grow on the High Plateau. Acacia, jujube trees, and grasses grow in the Sahara Desert.

A variety of animals live in Algeria, including wild boars and Barbary apes in the mountain regions and hyenas, gazelles, and jackals in the Sahara Desert. About four hundred kinds of birds live in Algeria.

History

Scientists believe people have lived in northern Africa for two hundred thousand years. The earliest settlers in what is now Algeria were known as the Berbers. In 800 B.C., the Phoenicians set up settlements along the North African coast, including Carthage. The Carthaginians lost their lands to the Romans in 146 B.C., and the Berber kingdoms began to grow. By A.D. 24, however, the Romans had taken over almost all Berber lands.

Left: This Algerian man is looking at a very old painting of a rhinoceros in a cave in Tassili n'Ajjer in the southeastern part of the Sahara Desert.

The Romans built grand cities, helped increase trade, and encouraged farming. The Berbers, however, were unhappy with Roman rule because the Romans took away their land to use for farming. In A.D. 429, the Vandals, a Christian Germanic group, took over the region. In A.D. 439, the Vandals took over Carthage. In A.D. 534, the Romans regained control of the area.

Above:
Roman ruins can still be found in the city of Timgad. The city was built by the Roman **emperor** Trajan (A.D. 53–117) and was originally called Thamugadi.

Arab Rule

In A.D. 642, Arabs began to take control of North Africa, including what is now Algeria. They brought the religion of Islam with them. The Ottomans took over in the 1400s. The local Ottoman rulers used **privateers** to raid European ships in the Mediterranean Sea. These raids angered Europe and the United States. In 1815, Algeria went to war against several European countries and the United States. Algeria lost the war and was forced to stop using privateers.

Fighting for Independence

By 1834, Algeria had become a French **colony**. French settlers took farmland and religious buildings from the local people. The locals became more and more unhappy with the French. In 1871, the Algerians fought against the French. The French stopped the fight, but the people of Algeria continued to **protest**.

After World War II, Algerian leaders set up a political party called the Front de Libération Nationale (FLN). The FLN declared war against the colonists and the French army in 1954. In 1962, Algeria was declared **independent**.

Left:
In 1960, Muslims, or followers of the religion of Islam, protested against French rule of Algeria. About sixty people were killed during the fighting.

13

Independent Algeria

Ahmed Ben Bella became Algeria's first president. He made Algeria a **socialist** state. In 1965, he was forced out of office by Houari Boumedienne.

In 1991, the Front Islamique du Salut (FIS), a political party that wanted to rule Algeria by strict Islamic law, won the elections. The Algerian army then took control. The FIS and its supporters **revolted**, and the fighting lasted eight years. Nearly one hundred thousand people were killed. In 1999, Abdelaziz Bouteflika was elected president.

Left: The bodies of people killed in a terrorist attack lie in coffins. The attack, which was carried out by an Islamic group, happened in a town near Algiers in 2001.

Abd al Qadir (1808–1883)

Abd al Qadir led the protest movement against French rule in the 1830s. He is regarded as a national hero.

Djamila Bouhired (1935–)

Djamila Bouhired fought for Algerian independence in the 1950s. She was captured by the French in 1957 and was sentenced to death, but she was put in jail instead. When Algeria became independent in 1962, she was released.

Djamila Bouhired

Ahmed Ben Bella (1918–)

Ahmed Ben Bella was elected the first president of Algeria in 1963. He was forced out of office because he misused his power.

Ahmed Ben Bella

Houari Boumedienne (1927–1978)

Houari Boumedienne became the second president of Algeria after he led a **coup** against Ahmed Ben Bella in 1965. During his time in office, he worked to improve the country's economy.

Houari Boumedienne

Government and the Economy

The president of Algeria is elected by the people for a five-year term. The president chooses the country's **prime minister** and a cabinet, or group of advisers. Algeria's **parliament** has two parts, the National People's Assembly and the Council of Nations. Voters elect the members of the National People's Assembly. Two-thirds of the members of the Council of Nations are elected by voters. The president chooses one-third.

Left: Abdelaziz Bouteflika (*far right*) waves to supporters during the 1999 election. He was reelected in 2004. As president, Bouteflika has a lot of power. He can break up Algeria's parliament without asking anyone else's permission.

Algeria's judicial system is based on Islamic religious law, socialism, and French law. The Supreme Court is the highest court in the country.

Local Government

Algeria has forty-eight *wilayat* (wee-LIE-yat), or **provinces**. Each province is governed by an assembly made up of thirty elected deputies and a *wali* (WAH-lee), or governor. The president chooses the walis. Each province's local government oversees education, farming, and tourism in the region.

The Economy

Most of Algeria's economy is based on its oil and gas industries. Much of the oil and gas is **exported** to the United States, Italy, Spain, and France. The country relies a lot on oil and gas for its income, so the economy does badly when oil and gas prices fall.

In 2003, a small number of Algerians worked in farming. Crops grown in the country include wheat, barley, oats, and olives. Algerian farmers cannot produce enough food, so some food is bought from other countries.

Above:
Most of Algeria's oil is pumped from three main oil fields that are located within the country.

Left:
Vegetables grown in Algeria are sold in markets throughout the country. Other fresh produce, such as grapes and citrus fruits, is also grown and sold in Algeria.

To help Algeria's economy become stable, the government has encouraged the growth of private businesses. The government has also tried to encourage foreign companies to put money into Algerian businesses not related to the oil and gas industries. Many foreign companies will not put money into Algerian businesses, however, because of violence in the country. As a result, many Algerians do not have jobs, and about one-fourth of Algerians are poor.

Above: The port in Algiers is one of the largest ports in the country. Algeria has thirteen ports in all.

People and Lifestyle

The population of Algeria is fairly young. In 2004, about one-third of all Algerians were under age fifteen. In the past, some Roman, French, and Arab people married Berbers. Because of these marriages, almost all Algerians are descendants of the Berbers. Most Algerians consider themselves to be Arabs, however.

Below: Some elderly Algerian men sit on a bench to talk. Most men in Algeria live to about the age of sixty-nine. Most women live to about the age of seventy-two.

Left: Algeria's cities are very crowded. Algerians who move to the cities to find jobs and a better way of life are often forced to live in shantytowns, which are poor areas in a town made up of rundown shacks or temporary homes.

City Life

Today, about half of Algeria's population lives in the country's cities. Most of these cities are located along the coast in the northern part of the country. Algiers, Algeria's capital and its largest city, is located in this area.

Every year, many Algerians move to the cities from the countryside to find work and improve their way of life. As a result, many of the country's cities are becoming more and more crowded, and there are fewer jobs.

Family Life

The family is at the center of Algerian life. Often, many family members live in the same house or very close to one another. It is **traditional** for the oldest man in the household to make all of the main decisions. In cities, however, the traditional roles are changing. In many parts of the countryside, men are still the heads of the households and work outside the home, while the women are in charge of the home and the children.

Below: In Algeria's cities, most public housing is only big enough for parents and their children. The smaller homes are changing the country's tradition of living in large family groups.

Left: These women and children walk along a street in the city of Bab el-Oued. Until recent years, families in Algeria have been large, with as many as eight children. Today, the size of most families in Algeria is smaller, with only two to three children.

Women and Marriage

Many marriages in Algeria are arranged by family members. Before a couple can get married, the families must agree to the terms of the marriage. Weddings often last several days. After she is married, a woman leaves her family and moves into her husband's home.

Due to the shortage of houses and jobs, many Algerian men cannot afford to get married. As a result, Algerians are getting married at a later age.

Below: Algeria's civil laws give women many of the same rights as men. The Family Code gives women few rights, however. The code is based on Islamic law and governs much of Algerian society.

Education

Since Algeria became independent, the government has worked to improve the education system. Today, education is free for all Algerian children.

All children in Algeria must attend primary and middle school for nine years. After middle school, they may attend high school, where they receive general, specialized, or **vocational** training. Students must pass an exam to graduate from high school. They may then attend a university, **technical** school, or vocational training center.

Left: Children in Algeria begin primary school at age six. Classes are taught in the Arabic language. Later, they learn French as a second language. Children in public schools also study Islam.

Algeria has ten universities. The best-known universities in the nation include the University of Oran, the University of Constantine, and the University of Algiers. Some Algerian students, however, choose to study in other countries.

Above: Before Algeria became independent, all of the teachers in Algeria's schools were from France. Today, most of the country's teachers are Algerian.

Education for Women

Today, Algerian girls in cities get the same level of education as boys. Most girls in the countryside, however, attend fewer years of school than boys.

Religion

Islam is the official religion of Algeria. The religion was first brought to North Africa by the Arabs. Today, almost all Algerians are Muslims, or followers of the Islamic religion.

Muslims live by a set of rules that are known as the Five Pillars of Islam. The rules are to declare their faith in God and Muhammad, pray five times a day, give money to the poor, fast during the holy month of **Ramadan**, and make a **pilgrimage** to the holy city of Mecca.

Above: These men are praying at one of the many mosques, or Muslim houses of worship, all over Algeria. Muslims must pray five times a day.

Other Beliefs

Of the small number of Algerians who are not Muslims, Christians make up the largest group. Christianity was first introduced to the country by the Romans. Most Christian Algerians are Roman Catholic, but a small number are followers of the Protestant faith. The country's Christian communities either attend church or hold religious services at home. Less than one hundred Jews live in Algeria.

Left:
The cathedral of Notre Dame d'Afrique is in the city of Algiers. The country's Christian communities live in the large cities of Algiers, Oran, and Constantine.

Language

Arabic is Algeria's official language. It is used in government and in the media. According to Algerian law, the Arabic language should be used in all parts of public life. Many Algerians can also speak French, but only a small number of the population can read and write French. Some people speak Tamazight or a form of the language. Tamazight is the Berbers' main language. It is also an official language of Algeria.

Below: Street signs in Algeria are written in both Arabic and French.

Literature

In the past, stories were told out loud and passed from one generation to the next in that way. In the 1800s, French settlers introduced the novel to Algerian literature. Since then, Algerian authors have written about colonial rule, the country's fight for independence, and Islam. Author Mouloud Feraoun wrote about the Berbers and their **culture**. Other famous Algerian writers include Albert Camus and Assia Djebar.

Arts

Music

Algerian music has been influenced by many other cultures. The Berbers have a strong musical tradition. Their music usually consists of people singing to the beat of one drum. In some Berber groups, women sing in high-pitched voices while people clap. Another kind of traditional music consists of wind instruments played in haunting tones.

Below: This Berber is playing a traditional stringed instrument in the town of Tindouf. Apart from desert music, Berbers also perform folk music, which they sing in their own language.

Chaabi (CHA-bee) is a type of Arab folk music that started in Algiers. Popular themes for chaabi songs include love, duty, and how life has changed in Algeria. El Hajj Muhammad El Anka, who died in 1978, was one of Algeria's best-known chaabi musicians.

Rai (RYE) is another popular kind of music. It is based on traditional folk music in which poems are sung. It has a strong beat that is easy to dance to. One famous rai singer is Cheb Khaled.

Above:
Lounés Matoub is a well-known Berber musician. He used his music to protest against the Algerian government's attempts to do away with Berber culture. He moved to France in 1978 but was killed during a visit to Algeria in 1998.

Architecture

Because of Algeria's past rulers, the nation has a rich architectural history. The country has Roman ruins, Arab mosques, Turkish palaces, and French cathedrals. The city of Algiers is known for its beautiful buildings. The Kasbah, an area within Algiers, is famous for its narrow, winding streets with many tall, flat-topped buildings. The town of El Oued is also famous. It is called the "Town of a Thousand Domes" because of its many dome-roofed clay houses.

Above: The Arch of Trajan is one of the Roman ruins in the city of Timgad. The Romans built many cities throughout Algeria and North Africa. Some of these cities can still be seen today.

Crafts

Algerian crafts include **embroidery**, metalwork, pottery, carpet making, and jewelry making. Carpets in Algeria are made in the same way they were made long ago. The carpets are made in many bright colors. The patterns used in the rugs are different from region to region.

Jewelry making has been influenced by the Berbers and the Arabs. Beautiful pieces are often made using traditional methods passed down by the Ottomans.

Left: This Algerian woman is weaving a carpet on a loom. Algerian carpets are made of sheep's wool, goats' hair, or camels' hair. They are used as prayer rugs, bath rugs, foot rugs, and blankets.

Leisure

In traditional Algerian society, men and women are not encouraged to mix with one another. As a result, women tend to visit female friends and family members at their homes.

Algerian men often go to cafés where they drink tea or coffee, meet friends, talk, and play board games such as chess, checkers, or dominoes.

Below: Cafés are popular places for men to get together and talk.

Left: Algerian women spend a lot of their time telling stories to their children or grandchildren. Storytelling is very popular in Algeria and helps keep historical and important family events alive.

Some Algerian men also like to spend their free time relaxing in public baths known as *hammams*.

Horse and camel racing are popular among Algerians who live in the desert. Other popular activities include camel dancing, which is moving camels to the beat of traditional music. In some parts of the desert, skiing on sand is popular.

Sports

Soccer is the most popular sport in Algeria. The country's national team has performed well in international competitions, including the World Cup and the African Nations Cup. One of Algeria's best-known soccer players is Zinedine Zidane. Descended from the Berbers, Zidane has played for both French and Spanish clubs. He was voted Player of the Year by the Fédération Internationale de Football Association (FIFA) in 1998, 2000, and 2003.

Below: These young boys are playing soccer in the street. Soccer is the most popular sport in Algeria, and Algerians love playing and watching the game.

Left: In 1991, Hassiba Boulmerka was the first African female to win a gold medal at the World Athletics Championships. The following year, she became the first Algerian to win a gold medal at the Olympics in Barcelona, Spain.

Sports Competitions

A number of Algerian athletes have performed well in track-and-field and boxing competitions with other nations. Hassiba Boulmerka and Noureddine Morceli, well-known Algerian runners, have won gold medals at the Olympics in the 1,500-meter event. At the 1996 Summer Olympics in Atlanta, Georgia, Hocine Soltani became the first person from Algeria to win a gold medal in boxing in the lightweight category.

Holidays and Festivals

Many holidays celebrated in Algeria are religious. The Muslim festival of Eid al-Seghir marks the end of Ramadan. Eid al-Kebir is celebrated at the end of the Islamic year. This festival honors Abraham's willingness to kill his son on God's orders. As part of the festivities, families kill a sheep and share the meat with relatives, friends, and the poor.

Below: Muslim Berbers gather to pray on the morning of Eid al-Kebir.

Apart from religious holy days, the country also has national holidays and local festivals. Revolution Day takes place on November 1. This day marks the start of the Algerian War of Independence. July 5 is Independence Day and celebrates the country's break with France. Local Algerian festivals are known as *moussem* (MOO-sem). Often, these festivals celebrate the harvests of different types of crops.

Food

The main food in Algeria is couscous, which is usually made of semolina, or hard wheat, grain. It is mostly eaten with meat or vegetables and gravy.

Stews are popular dishes. Common stews include *shakshuka* (shak-SHOO-ka), a vegetable stew; *tajine* (tah-JEEN), a lamb or chicken stew; and *chorba* (CHOR-ba), a spicy stew made with lamb or chicken, herbs, and vegetables.

Below:
These women are making couscous. In northern Algeria, couscous is made from semolina, or hard wheat. In the south, couscous is made of a mixture of soft wheat, rye, and barley grains.

Other favorite dishes are *burek* (BOO-rek), a mixture of egg, meat, and onion in pastry; meat-stuffed vegetables; and spicy lamb sausages.

Pastries are also popular, especially pastries filled with almonds and honey. Some pastries contain figs and dates, while other pastries are made of rose water, semolina, and butter.

Favorite drinks include sweet, strong coffee and mint-flavored tea. Fruit-based drinks are also popular.

Above:
Brochettes are a type of kebob that are eaten with French bread.

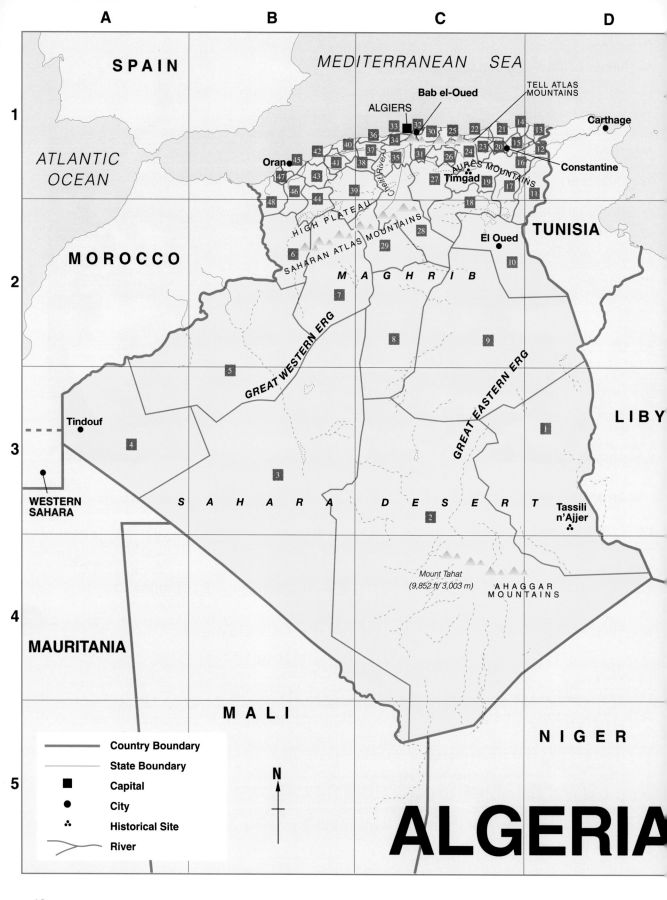

ALGERIA

Map Labels

SPAIN

MEDITERRANEAN SEA

TELL ATLAS MOUNTAINS

Bab el-Oued

ALGIERS

Carthage

ATLANTIC OCEAN

Oran

Constantine

AURES MOUNTAINS

Timgad

MOROCCO

HIGH PLATEAU

SAHARAN ATLAS MOUNTAINS

El Oued

TUNISIA

M A G H R I B

GREAT WESTERN ERG

GREAT EASTERN ERG

LIBY

Tindouf

WESTERN SAHARA

S A H A R A   D E S E R T

Tassili n'Ajjer

MAURITANIA

Mount Tahat
(9,852 ft / 3,003 m)

A H A G G A R
M O U N T A I N S

M A L I

N I G E R

Chelif River

Map Legend

▬▬▬	Country Boundary
▬	State Boundary
■	Capital
●	City
⁘	Historical Site
∿	River

N

Provinces

1. Illizi
2. Tamanghasset
3. Adrar
4. Tindouf
5. Bechar
6. Naama
7. El Bayadh
8. Ghardaïa
9. Ouargla
10. El Oued
11. Tebessa
12. Souk Ahras
13. El Tarf
14. Annaba
15. Guelma
16. Oum el Bouaghi
17. Khenchela
18. Biskra
19. Batna
20. Constantine
21. Skikda
22. Jijel
23. Mila
24. Setif
25. Bejaia
26. Bordj Bou Arreridj
27. M' Sila
28. Djelfa
29. Laghouat
30. Tizi Ouzou
31. Bouira
32. Bourmerdes
33. Alger
34. Blida
35. Medea
36. Tipaza
37. Ain Defla
38. Tissemsilt
39. Tiaret
40. Chlef
41. Relizane
42. Mostaganem
43. Mascara
44. Saida
45. Oran
46. Sidi Bel Abbes
47. Ain Temouchent
48. Tlemcen

Above: A man sells colorful Algerian carpets at a market.

Ahaggar Mountains C4–D4
Algiers C1
Atlantic Ocean A1–A2
Aurès Mountains C1–D1

Bab el-Oued C1

Carthage D1
Chelif River B1–C2
Constantine C1

El Oued C2

Great Eastern Erg C2–D4
Great Western Erg A3–B4

High Plateau B2–C2

Libya D2–D4

Mali A3–C5
Mauritania A3–A5
Mediterranean Sea B1–D2
Morocco A1–B2
Mount Tahat C4

Niger C5–D5

Oran B1

Sahara Desert B2–D4

Saharan Atlas Mountains B2–C2
Spain A1–B1

Tassili n'Ajjer D3
Tell Atlas Mountains C1
Timgad C1
Tindouf A3
Tunisia D1–D2

Western Sahara A3

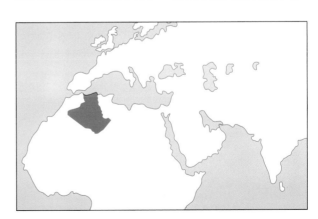

Quick Facts

Official Name	People's Democratic Republic of Algeria
Capital	Algiers
Official Language	Arabic
Population	32,129,324 (July 2004 estimate)
Land Area	919,595 square miles (2,381,740 square km)
Provinces	Adrar, Ain Defla, Ain Temouchent, Alger, Annaba, Batna, Bechar, Bejaia, Biskra, Blida, Bordj Bou Arreridj, Bouira, Bourmerdes, Chlef, Constantine, Djelfa, El Bayadh, El Oued, El Tarf, Ghardaïa, Guelma, Illizi, Jijel, Khenchela, Laghouat, Mascara, Medea, Mila, Mostaganem, M' Sila, Naama, Oran, Ouargla, Oum el Bouaghi, Relizane, Saida, Setif, Sidi Bel Abbes, Skikda, Souk Ahras, Tamanghasset, Tebessa, Tiaret, Tindouf, Tipaza, Tissemsilt, Tizi Ouzou, Tlemcen
Border Countries	Libya, Mali, Mauritania, Morocco, Niger, Tunisia
Highest Point	Mount Tahat 9,852 feet (3,003 m)
Major River	Chelif
Official Religion	Islam
Currency	Algerian dinar (71.65 DZD= U.S. $1 in 2005)

Opposite: This young Muslim girl in Algeria is holding the Koran, the Islamic holy book.

Glossary

cathedral: an important or large church, usually with lots of decorations.

colony: a village set up in one country but controlled by another country.

coup: a violent political fight that results in a change of government.

culture: the customs, beliefs, language, and arts of one group or country.

descendants: people born in a recent generation to one group or family.

embroidery: the art of decorating cloth or clothes with fancy sewing.

emperor: a person who rules an empire, which is a large collection of lands.

erg: a very large area of sand in a desert.

exported (v): sold and shipped from one country to another country.

extinct: no longer existing or living.

independent: regarding being free of control by others.

native: belonging to a land or region by having first grown or been born there.

nomad: a person who moves from place to place and who often lives in a tent.

parliament: a government group that makes the laws for their country.

pilgrimage: a journey made to a holy place as an act of religious devotion.

plateau: a wide, flat area of land that is surrounded by lower land.

prime minister: the highest government adviser under a ruler or president.

privateers: private ships allowed by the government to attack enemy ships.

protest (v): to argue strongly against someone or something.

provinces: regions of a country with set borders and their own local officials.

purity: being pure or without sin.

Ramadan: ninth month of the Islamic calendar. Muslims do not drink or eat during daytime hours that month.

revolted: fought, most often violently, against the government.

socialist: regarding a society in which the government owns all property and controls the economy.

technical: relating to using machines or science to perform a job or task.

traditional: regarding customs or styles passed down through the generations.

vocational: relating to a job, profession, or skilled trade.

More Books to Read

Algeria. Modern Nations of the World series. Tony Zurlo (Lucent Books)

I Am Muslim. Religions of the World series. Jessica Chalfonte (Powerkids Press)

Muslim Mosque. Places of Worship series. Angela Wood (Gareth Stevens)

Peoples of the Desert. People and Their Environments series. Robert Low (PowerKids Press)

Ramadan. On My Own Holidays series. Susan Douglass (Lerner Publishing)

The Sabbath Lion: A Jewish Folktale from Algeria. Howard Schwartz (HarperCollins Children's Books)

The Sahara Desert: The Biggest Desert. Great Record Breakers in Nature series. Aileen Weintraub. (PowerKids Press)

Tuaregs. Endangered Cultures series. Ann Carey Sabbah (Smart Apple Media)

Videos

Lost Treasures of the Ancient World 2: The Romans in North Africa (Kultur Video)

Sahara: A Place of Extremes (PBS Home Video)

Web Sites

cyberschoolbus.un.org/infonation/ index.asp?id=12

ladywildlife.com/animal/ barbaryape.html

www.enchantedlearning.com/africa/ algeria/flag/

www.pbs.org/wnet/africa/explore/ sahara/sahara_overview_lo.html

Due to the dynamic nature of the Internet, some web sites stay current longer than others. To find additional web sites, use a reliable search engine with one or more of the following keywords to help you locate information about Algeria. Keywords: *Algiers, Berbers, Albert Camus, Constantine, Kasbah, Sahara Desert, Tuaregs.*

Index